THE TRUE MEANING OF CHRISTMAS

To: AlIVIA
Love: Great Aunt
Carole
Christmas 2011

THE TRUE MEANIN

Text by Archbishop Fulton J. Sheen

F CHRISTMAS

Illustrations by FRITZ KREDEL

NIHIL OBSTAT:

John M. A. Fearns, S.T.D., Censor Librorum

IMPRIMATUR:

Francis Cardinal Spellman, Archbishop of New York

NEW YORK: September 6, 1955

ISBN: 978-1-934888-08-7

Roman Catholic Books

P. O. Box 2286 • Fort Collins, CO 80522
*Books*for*Catholics.com*

Printed in Mexico

DEDICATED

TO

THE MOTHER OF CHRISTMAS

THE VIRGIN MARY

THAT

SHE MAY FORM CHRIST

THE SON OF GOD IN US

AS THE SPIRIT FORMED

CHRIST IN HER

There are only two philosophies of life: one, the pagan; the other, the Judaic-Christian. In all pagan religions man tries to climb to God. In the Judaic-Christian tradition, God comes to man: by revelation to the prophets for the Jews, in the flesh for the Christians in the person of Jesus Christ the Son of God.

In religions such as Buddhism, Confucianism, Hinduism and the like, man is the wooer and God the wooed; man the seeker, God the found. In the Judaic-Christian tradition, the role of man to God is that of mirror to light, echo to voice. What has revealed the love of God where we are concerned, is that He has sent His Only Begotten Son into the world so that we might have life through Him. That love resides not in our showing any love for God, but in His showing love for us first, when He sent out His Son to be atonement for our sins, and therefore our Saviour.

God loved us first. God's love for us is not affirmed because we seek Him or reach out to Him and He responds to us. God does not love us because we are lovely or loveable; His love exists not on account of

our character, but on account of His. Our highest experience is responsive, *not initiative; God loves, we are loved.*

It is true that as men mount in knowledge and in virtue, it seems as if God begins then to love them; this is only because they are now, for the first time, sensitive to His love, or because they removed the barriers that kept the love of God from shining upon them. A man who is blind from birth, having had an operation on his eyes which restored his sight, might think that the sun was just beginning to shine in the heavens and the flowers just beginning to bloom. But all of these things existed since the beginning although his eyes were not in the condition to see them. Every child at the age of six or seven begins to be conscious of his mother's love, but the mother bestowed love on her child before the child was born; the maternal solicitude and love existed before her portals of the flesh were thrown open or the child was conscious of affection. In like manner, all the yearnings we have for good are the crying out of the soul for God under the influence of His love for us. Every demand for the spiritual comes from God, Whose Finger stirs our soul.

As the chemicals have no right to say there is no life above them, and the rose has no right to say there is no life above it, so man has a duty in his rational moments to recognize that there is a Higher Life above the human. But if our human life is

ever to be lifted up, be incorporated into the Divine, God must in some way come down to us. Chemicals are taken up into plants; plant life is absorbed by animal life; animal life is incorporated by the human. Shall not the human be lifted to the Divine?

But, plants can assimilate chemicals and animals can consume plants and man can take animals unto himself without consultation. These things are appropriated by sheer force. But God, having made man free, will not destroy his freedom. There will be no confiscation of humanity by Divinity. If man is ever to be taken up into the Divine Order there will have to be a free act on the part of man. God comes to man, not to devour him, but to consult him.

One day there came out from the great white throne of light an angel of light, descending down over the Plains of Esdrelon, coming to a Virgin kneeling in prayer, saying to Her in the Name of God: "Will you give Me a human nature? Speaking in the name of all humanity will you by an act of freedom say, 'Here is a man.'?" The woman answered, "Fiat": "be it done." The woman's role is submission and surrender. Here woman was playing her greatest role, surrendering herself to God.

But no human nature could ever be formed in her womb without fire and love and passion. There are other fires than those of the flesh and other passions than those of men. The fire and the passion and the love that descended upon Her was the Spirit and the Flame and the Love of God Himself.

Nine months passed. One night there rang out over the stillness of an evening breeze, out over the white chalked hills of Bethlehem—a gentle cry. The sea did not hear the voice, for the sea was filled with its own voice. The great ones of the earth did not hear the cry, for they could not understand how a Child could be greater than a man. There were only two classes of people who heard the cry that night: shepherds and wise men. Shepherds: those who know they know nothing. Wise men: those who know they do not know everything. Only the very simple and the very learned discovered God—never the man with one book.

When the shepherds and wise men came to the Crib, they saw a Babe Whose tiny hands were not quite long enough to touch the huge heads of the cattle, and yet were the hands that were steering the sun and moon and stars in their courses. They saw Baby Feet that did not walk, and yet one day would bear the weight of Divine Omnipotence; they saw eyes that might have read the secrets of every living heart that hour; under the Baby Brow they knew was beating a mind and an intelligence that fashioned the universe and with it a human intelligence that would grow in age and grace and wisdom before God and man.

This Babe Who is named Jesus, which means Saviour, is not a man who

made himself a God; nor is He an ethical reformer like Confucius, nor a teacher like Socrates, nor one who would develop into a greater consciousness of His Godhead as time went on. But rather He is true God and true Man, for He did not cease being God when He became Man. There was no conversion of His Godhead into flesh, but the taking up of manhood unto God.

When we say that God became Man, we do not mean that the Godhead was cut down to human dimensions; it means, on the contrary, that a human nature was taken up into the Person of God and made One with Him. This union is called the Incarnation, which literally means an "enfleshment," or "made flesh."

"There was not room in the inn."

Out to the hillside, to a stable cave, where shepherds drove their flocks in storms, Joseph and Mary go for shelter. There, in a place of peace and tranquility, in the utter abandonment and cold of a windswept cave; there, under the floor of the world, Mary, as a flesh and blood ciborium, lifts up, to the gaze of all, the Host of the world. "Behold the Lamb of God Who taketh away the sins of the world." He Who was born without a mother in heaven is born without a father on earth.

Of every other child born into the world, friends might say that it resembles its mother. This is the first instance in time that anyone could say that the Mother resembles the Child. Here is the beautiful par-

*adox of the Child Who made His Mother;
therefore, the Mother is only a child—a
creature of God. It was also the first time in
the history of this earth of ours that anyone
could ever think of heaven being anywhere
else than "way up there," but Mary, with
the Divine Child in Her arms, now looks
down to Heaven.*

*The human nature which God as-
sumed, was taken out of the world of freedom by a free act on the part of Mary His
Mother. God's way with man is not dicta-
torship but cooperation. He would redeem
humanity with human consent, and not
against it.*

Christmas is not something that
happened *such as the Battle of Waterloo; it*

is something that is happening. *What happened to the human nature which Christ took from Mary by her consent, can happen, in a lesser manner, to our human nature, by our free consent.*

On our part, there must be the free response of man to the Divine initiative, but this implies dying to the lower existence of sin and selfishness, pride and lust. To become a Christian does not mean reading religious books, or singing hymns or being kind to neighbors; it means sharing the Divinity that first came to us at Bethlehem. We can conceive of our manhood being taken up into God, since God has humbled Himself to take our nature. When this Christ-life gets inside of us, it affects our intellect, by

*giving us a truth which reason itself can-
not know; it affects our will, by giving us
an impetus and an energy for good which
we could not produce of and by ourselves. It
is, in the truest sense of the term, a rebirth,
except this time we are born not of the flesh,
but of the Spirit. As someone has said, "We
are all eggs at present, but we just cannot
go on being ordinarily 'decent eggs.' Either
we have to get hatched to the Divine or
else we rot." The descent of God to man, and
eternity into time, makes a tremendous dif-
ference to all people whether they ever heard
of Him or not, or whether they respect Him
or not. From that point on, it is possible for
man to divinize himself, not by his own ef-
forts, but by response to Divine Life. Just as*

27

our modern world is bathed in radio and television waves but only those who are tuned in to them receive their messages of knowledge and enjoyment, so, too, there is a radiation through history of this Divine Life, but only those who freely appropriate it ever enjoy its peace and blessing. Once, however, we assent to the crucifixion of that which is low and base in us, His life can make the feeblest, filthiest of us blaze with a dazzling, radiant light so that we become as stainless mirrors that reflect the life of God. The process is not easy because the purpose of God's coming to man was not to make us nice *people, but to make us* new *creatures. If marble suddenly began to bloom, and flowers suddenly began to move*

from shade to sunshine, and dogs began to quote Shakespeare and Dante, they would be manifesting a power and a capacity which was quite beyond their nature; so, too, if we who are creatures of God, pieces of His own handiwork, began to be partakers of His Divine Nature and in the truest sense of the word His children, this would be something that transcends our nature far more than a marble blooming or a dog quoting poetry.

The power is there to make us different than we are; it is for our freedom to decide if we will respond, and if we are willing to pay the price of having the dross burned off the gold in the flames of love. Let it not be said by anyone, "I am too foul; I

am a beast; I am not worthy to be lifted up."
It was to assure just such persons as these
that He was born in a stable, and on His
first night in this world companioned with
beasts.